ISBN: 978-0-9893683-0-8

First Edition

THERE IS NO SAFETY

GRAHAM MURTAUGH

MIGRATORY

On the back porch
is not a dead bird.
You see blood
spilled, red drops
spotting the flower pot,
the flowers, a faint halo
on the window.
You see the softness
of its feathered head, iridescent
oils flaming as the sun comes on.
You see the new curve of
its neck, sharp
where God said *soft.*
Its wings wrapped tight.
You see but do not see
a dead bird. You see
its parts. You see
an assumption: dead, bird.
The bird has flown on,
is still heading south
for the winter.

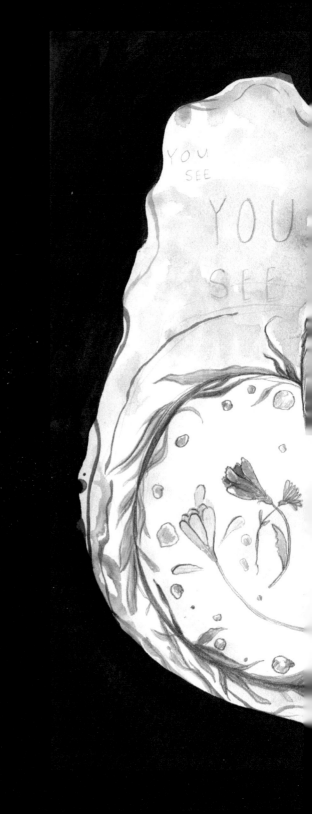

MY OTHER,

LONLIER BROTHER

My other, lonelier brother

is a digital hermit, bearded,
overweight, incisive, with arms
to crush you in a bear hug.

lives alone between the gun-grey Sound
and a Texaco, a pavement wedge walk-up
in the slip of Bremerton.

curses the TSA, taxes, Republicans,
bad drivers. When we go for walks
in my calm neighborhood, well-tended,
I am always looking over my shoulder,
embarrassed.

My other, lonelier brother

has forever beat me at chess, always
three moves ahead. I visit at Christmas,
make the drive in rain masquerading
as snow. I arrive late. The board is set.
We share slowly warming Krogstad.

worries my vanquished pawns
with absent clicks. He weeps quietly,
his burled beard glistening,
lamenting. *Fucking lamentations.*

My other, lonelier brother

and I don't agree on God,
though we share instinctively
the language of gnashing
of teeth, of sackcloth and ashes.

slides me the amber dregs. I drink
deep and look out on the Sound:
a trawler at night, its portals
lit, spilling like oil, flame
unfolding on the waves.

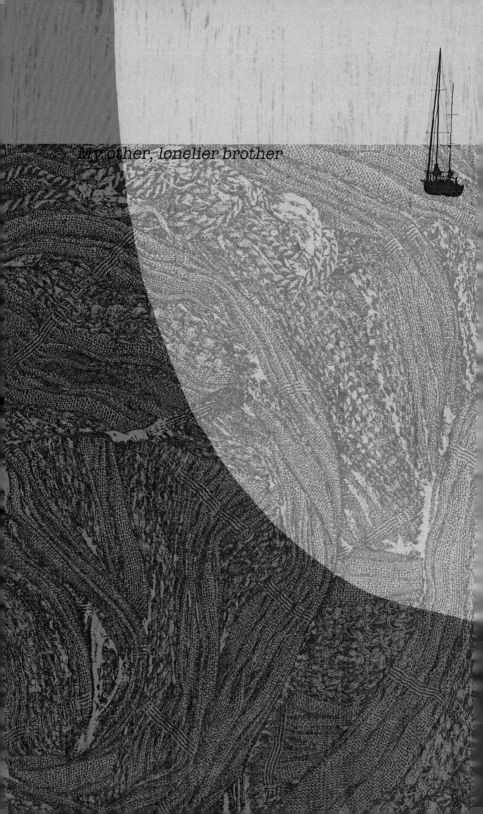

My other, lonelier brother

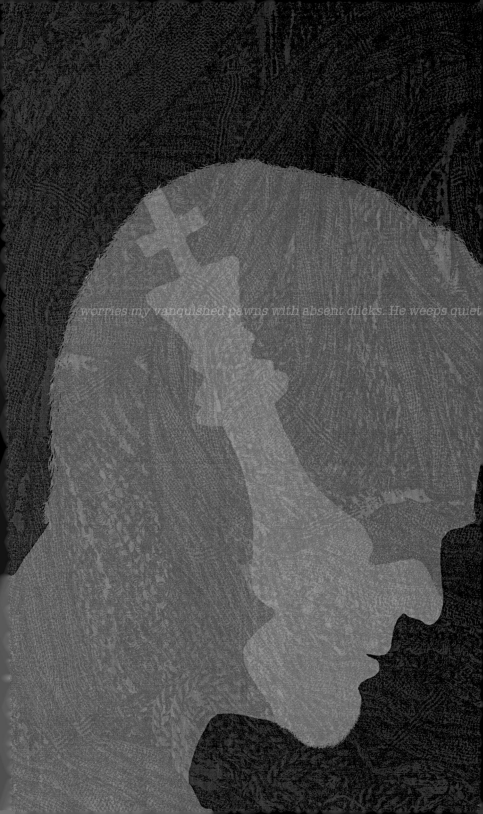

worries my vanquished pawns with absent clicks. He weeps quiet

INSOMNIA

I am having trouble sleeping
with you curled against me.
I can feel your dreams
shuddering, minnows
flitting through your veins.
Your spine's pilings
shift under my touch.
You are always falling
or failing to run. You are leaden.
You rest in the shape
of how I hold you.
I am careless
and don't hold you well.
There is no safety
in sleep. There should be.

DELTA RAY

MOTOR INN

Home

An inventory of Room 224 of the Delta Ray Motor Inn:
blue carpeting; a queen-sized bed with faded floral
bedspread and, depending on rotation, cigarette burns;
matching floral drapes; two shiny wooden end tables,
the drawers of which contain a Port County phone book
(lower) and Gideon Bible (upper); a white phone with a
red light bulb; two blue and gold lamps; a three-drawer
wooden dresser, on top of which is a 21-inch black and
white television; a sliding glass door that opens onto a
concrete balcony with white metal railings; a white min-
iature Kenmore refrigerator on top of which are two clear
plastic cups and a black plastic ice bucket; a rectangular
mirror in a gold frame above the bed; a second rectangular
mirror (unframed) in the yellow linoleum bathroom; white
tap handles and spigot; two off-white towels and match-
ing wash cloths; two miniature bars of soap, one shampoo,
one conditioner; a suction-footed bathmat, also yellow; an
Airtrans air conditioner; an amber-colored glass ashtray
with Delta Ray Motor Inn *etched on the bottom; an*
emergency exit map on the back of the front door.

Beyond the front door is an open-air covered walkway, dusted over with sand and small rocks and painted blue. In the parking lot, in sharp pink neon, the Delta Ray Motor Inn announces its VACANCY. *Then the north and south bound interstate and light poles at thirty-foot intervals in either direction. Out the sliding glass door, off the small balcony, is an empty field. Farther off is a stand of trees, of which only the tops are visible.*

The Businessman

There is a man who comes to my room every few weeks. He has been coming for years. His name is Noel Strunk. He is short and middle-aged and balding. He wears a brown suit that he hangs on a hook on the bathroom door. He idles around in his underwear and a white shirt, sometimes socks.

He carries a large leather bag. He takes things in and out of it, setting them on the bed, organizing them first by color, then size. He often has a piece of paper, a list, and he makes phone calls on the telephone and sometimes he picks up some of the things on the bed as he talks. He talks loudly on the phone, but when he is alone, he talks quietly to himself.

"Noel," he will say. "You're alright. You've got to put it together, though. This time, you've got to make it happen." And then he will pick up the phone and a deep voice will come out of him. "Noel Strunk," he will say and he will laugh and strut in his striped underwear up and down the blue carpet.

In the beginning, when I first knew him, he came with a woman. She had red lips and she smiled at Noel and Noel smiled at her. I watched them touch and laugh and couple. They were free in their love; others are not so free. Others are angry or violent or distant.

Noel and this woman came frequently. And then, for a long time, Noel did not come. And when he reappeared in my room, he was alone.

Noel arrived and arranged his things just so and then left. It was night and I could see the neon on the bedspread through the window. When Noel returned he looked as if he was dancing and he had a woman with him.

"This is it. Best room in the house."

The woman had dark glossy hair and she was plump, like Maria the maid.

"You have to pick your spots, you know." Noel pressed his fists into his back. "Smoke-free, away from the ice machine, near the back, upper floor. It's an art, really. I know all the best spots from here to San Diego."

"The best, huh?" the woman said. She was looking right at me.

"After sixteen years? I should. Absolutely!" Noel laughed loudly.

Noel and the woman stood right in front of me. He had his hands on her hips. They were eye to eye. She popped her gum.

"I could show you. The whole West Coast.

Here to San Diego. Heck, to Mexico."

"Yeah?"

The woman counted the money and then tucked it away in her shoe. She locked the door and turned off the light. The drapes were pulled, but the neon snuck in around the corners, bleeding to the edge of the bed. I could still see a little.

Name

There were three of them: the woman opening the drapes; the man dragging the overstuffed suitcase in through the door, huffing and puffing with the weight; the little red-headed boy looking around. He saw me and came over and stood, looking up.

He pointed. His mouth was open.

He said, "Billy!"

"No, sweetheart, that's not Billy."

"Make him sing!"

"Honey, that's not Billy. That's a real fish."

"It ain't even a bass," said the man.

"I wanna hear the song!"

"Nate, this isn't Billy. This fish doesn't sing. Understand?"

"Where's the button?" The boy's voice was shrill and his face seemed to collapse.

"Jesus."

"He's tired, Steve."

"*I'm* tired, Diane. You try driving seven hours stuck behind a goddamned semi."

"Billy!" The boy reached his pudgy hand towards me, his fingers spreading.

"Nate, honey, let's go to the pool, okay? You wanna go swimming? Get your trunks on."

The boy and the woman flip-flopped out the door and down the hallway. The man left the bathroom door open and I watched him stand to urinate. He flushed but did not wash his hands. He opened all the drawers and walked onto the small balcony and threw the Gideon Bible into the empty field. He leaned over the edge and spat then walked inside and looked at me. He came over and leaned close. He had a mustache and small brown eyes.

"Singing fish, my ass," he said.

He reached toward me and I lost his hands and the world spun and I stared down at his bare feet. His toes scrunched in the blue carpet.

"China. I knew it." He flipped me around.

"Oughta name you Birry Ree."

The Maids

Veronica was young and did not waddle like the older women. Josefina was in charge then. And then Josefina was gone and it was Diadora, and then Svetlana from Minsk, and then Maria, and Maria again, until Veronica was finally Head of Housekeeping. By then Veronica had three children and had lost a husband and remarried. All this I learned while the women cleaned, stripping sheets and watching *telanovelas*, slowly vacuuming back and forth

"This is the best room," Veronica said to Maria. She was young and new to me. "It is far from the desk and you may smoke on the balcony. *Pero tenga prisa.* Do not come here with Señor Kyle. *¿Me entiendes?*"

In the end it happened to Maria, too. One night when all I could see were headlights sweeping along the highway, the door opened a coffin of light on the carpet.

"*Pase,*" a man's voice said. For a moment after the door closed the light was shut out and I could only hear breathing. A hand moved the drapes apart, letting in a fuzzy light. Mr. Kyle guarded the door. Maria stood near the bed, across the room. She kept her arms crossed in front of her.

Mr. Kyle wore slacks and a pink shirt like the men who set their golf clubs next to the refrigerator. Tan with curly brown hair, he wore brown leather shoes and a belt that matched. He watched Maria, who looked at the floor, and moved his tongue inside his mouth.

"You understand the situation. *¿Sí?*"

Maria did not answer him.

"*Mírame.*" Mr. Kyle sounded like Grigorio, the murderous banker from *Paso a Paso.* Maria looked up.

"You understand? *¿Sí o no?*"

"*Sí.*"

"*¿Entonces?*"

Maria nodded slowly, her hair falling in her face.

"*Dime.*"

"*Sí.*"

The drapes swept closed. There was the metallic clink of a belt and then the hiss and shuffle of fabric piling on the floor. The bed springs creaked. Then Maria began to speak. I could not understand without her lips to watch.

"*¿Estás orando? ¿A qué dios?*" Mr. Kyle said and laughed loud in the darkness. I knew how it would go for them.

The door opened forcefully. Light fell across Mr. Kyle, naked and hunched in the middle of the bed. Maria was pushed up against the headboard, wrapped around herself. They both stared, Mr. Kyle over his shoulder.

For a moment, the only sound was the large key ring jingling in the doorknob.

The gunshot was loud. Mr. Kyle lurched and fell off the bed. There was no other sound.

"*Hija,*" a voice said. "*Venga.*"

Maria stood and stepped to the door, walking quickly past the window.

A head entered the door of light. It was Veronica. She spat twice on the carpet and then turned and disappeared down the stairs.

Samuel

Samuel is the maintenance man. He shuffles and has big hands, which he wraps around hammers or a red toolbox. He has fixed the Airtrans unit many times, taking pieces apart and setting them on a brown plastic tarp. He is careful not to stain the bedspread or curtains with oil. He wears overalls with his name stitched on the front.

In the evenings when no one is in my room, Samuel lets himself in and sits on the balcony in the sunset and smokes cigarettes. I can hear him talking, with the door open, but cannot always hear what he says. Sometimes he sits on the edge of the bed and prays and talks to Beatrice, who is dead. He cries and covers his red face. A little curl of gray hair flops down across his hands and shakes.

Sometimes Samuel sleeps on the top of the bed, his hands clasped on his chest, his mouth shut tight. He does not move.

Most people struggle in their sleep. They shift and roll, murmuring, talking out loud. Their hands flutter or they kick their legs. Sometimes they wake up the people they are with, but most often not. Two people are active all night and do not know it. When there are children present—on a cot or on the floor—it can be a very busy room, with all kinds of moving.

But when a woman wakes from her dream or a child needs a cup of water, the movement ceases. All is quiet and still. The freeway rustles. And then, when everyone is asleep again, it resumes. As if something is waiting.

Youth

    "Micah, turn off the light."

    "Come on, Nadine. It's okay."

    "Turn it off, please."

    "Nadine."

    An hour before, the boy had kicked the door open, struggling to carry the girl inside, dumping her on the bed. They laughed and kissed, rolling on the unwashed bedspread; the maids only ever change the sheets. After a while they separated, lying side by side. The girl took the boy's hand, holding it up, staring at the long fingers.

    "Mrs. Micah Peach."

    "Amen."

    The girl turned a thin silver ring around his finger. "They'll be upset."

    "We'll be alright."

    "I know."

    "And I'll get you a real diamond. Soon."

    "What about a place?"

    "Okay, that too." The boy's long fingers brushed along the girl's throat, under her chin. "But: first things first, oh flesh of my flesh."

    "Micah." She brushed his hand away.

"I'm serious."

"So am I."

The boy sat up onto his knees and turned toward the girl. He pulled out of his shirt. In the mirror the girl ran a hand along a scar on his chest, pressing her palm there.

"What if it happens again?"

"It won't."

"I'll be a widow at twenty-two."

"Come on. This is supposed to be our night."

He bent over her, hiding her in the curve of his body. His skin was pale. They never turned the light off, as most do, even when things became strained and uncertain. Their movement stalled and they separated. The boy stroked the girl's brow, along the hairline. I could not hear what he whispered. After a while, he got up and turned out the light.

They settled into darkness. Their breathing slowed. Neon pressed against the drapes.

Feet hushed on the carpet. The boy stepped into the moonlight coming through the sliding glass door. He stood in front of his own image and rubbed a thumb down the long scar. For a moment, he was lit up all white, then just as quickly he was dropped back into shadow.

Noel

It has been months since I have seen Noel Strunk. Once,

before, he came with his son.

"Quite a place, eh, Daniel," Noel said. Daniel was thick and slouched like his father. He read comic books while Noel made phone calls.

Suddenly, Noel erupted.

"I just sold the sonofabitch 30 cases! How about your old man? Let's go celebrate! I'm gonna buy you a steak the size of your face!"

"Why do you do that?" Daniel said, glancing up.

"Do what, son?" Noel smiled with his yellow teeth. He wore his white shirt and faded candy-striped boxers.

"That voice. That's not your real voice."

"It's my Salesman Voice," Noel said, pulling a face. "All salesmen have one."

"Sounds fake." Daniel went back to his comics. "Let's get pizza."

Now Noel is alone. He does not open the windows or turn on the air conditioner—"Listen to that baby hum!"—though it is August. He lies on the bed, fully clothed, and stares at the ceiling. When the light is nearly gone, Noel gets up and leaves. He does not lock the door.

Noel returns with paper bag inside of which is an amber bottle. Noel collects the ice bucket and leaves the room again. The door is open and I can see the empty highway. A car appears and I watch until its red lights vanish.

Noel fills a plastic cup with ice and pours from the bottle. He takes a ballpoint pen inscribed with the name of the Delta Ray Motor Inn and a small pad of paper from the nightstand and begins to write, sitting on the edge of the bed. The pages are small and they tear off and scatter on the bed and floor. It is silent except for the sound of Noel's writing and the crinkle of the cup in his hand. When he is done, he gathers the pages and sets them on the dresser, next to the television. He puts the pen on top. He places the empty bottle just to the left and leans against the television.

He is close. His eyes are red and glazed and his face is wet. He has sweated through his shirt, the stains deep and yellow, like his teeth. He wipes a hairy wrist across his forehead. He breathes heavily and says "Hoo, boy."

He undresses, folding his pants neatly and placing them in the top drawer. He bunches his socks and puts them in his shoes, which he also places in the top drawer. He is in a white shirt and solid blue underwear. His suit jacket hangs from the bathroom door. He reaches into a jacket pocket and retrieves a tiny orange bottle with a white lid.

I have seen this before. On television a hundred times and once, when a trio—two young women and a man—met in my room. They also had small orange bottles. The television was loud and the three laughed and one of the young women laid down. They slapped and shook her. They yelled into the phone that she would not wake up and then they carried her out of the room. They did not return.

Noel shakes the contents of the bottle out. White ovals mound in his hand. Noel stares at them, standing in his underwear in the middle of the room. He seems to be counting them, looking intently at each individual oval.

"Hoo, boy," he says again.

Time

The Midland Railway Desk Clock had a white face with black numbers and three revolving black arms, each one longer than the next. On the right side were silver numbers on plates. Each midnight a new plate fell into place with a soft click.

One summer an older couple—the man in a white floppy hat with *Palm Springs* stitched across the front, the woman with a fleshy neck—checked in. The man walked slow circles around the room, gently touching the bed, the dresser and out to the balcony to stare at the dried weeds. Once in a while the woman would say *George, rest a minute* and he would sit on the bed and move the arms of the Midland Railway before starting over. In the evening they watched game shows, the sliding glass door open to the night air and the sound of the freeway.

In the morning while the woman showered, the man unplugged the Midland Railway Desk Clock. He wrapped it in a green sweater and put in the bottom of his suitcase. It left a fine dust shadow behind. When the woman came out of the bathroom, he was watching cartoons.

Now I watch the changes of light across the bedspread, glinting off the mirrors, slowly filling in the corners. I hear feet approach on the walkway and the doors of distant rooms opening and closing. The voices are muted, but sometimes I can tell what television show is on by the music or the actor's intonation.

If no one stays in my room, it is not cleaned. *¡Que lastima!* the maids will say when they arrive. The dust will have piled, falling out of the air. If it has been a very long time, they will open the doors and wind will sweep in, bringing sound and a different kind of light. The maids will vacuum and fluff the pillows and turn on the television. I know that soon someone will be coming to stay.

Sometimes, no one comes. My room glistens from the polish, and only I am here to see it.

But I am not alone. In the field there are tiny flowers mixed in with the dead grass. Black birds land in groups. And there is a small animal, brown like the field, except for his feet which are white as the tip of his tail. He stays far from the white chairs and tables on the ground floor.

I see him most often in early morning, just before full light when the freeway is quiet. He stalks, nosing the garbage wilting in the field. Sometimes he will pause, sniffing the air, looking from side to side. He waits, one white foot raised to his chest, frozen. The wind ruffles the fur along his back. He never looks up.

No Vacancy

Mr. Kyle went still. The door was open to the parking lot and the lines of neon from the Delta Ray Motor Inn reflected in his eyes.

Bands of light grew and the clouds changed colors. The billboard with the smiling young woman came out of the darkness.

Later I heard footsteps on the stairs. The light was gray. Samuel blinked, his big hands on the door.

"Jesus."

Police cars arrived and an ambulance. Guests gathered in the parking lot. They held their arms over their chests.

Mr. Kyle left a stain that could not be cleaned. For two days men stepped gingerly through my room taking pictures, talking in low voices with one another. They made jokes and smoked out on the walkway, watching traffic.

A group of men in white suits arrived some days later. They took all the linens and put them in individual plastic bags and labeled them. They cut out the carpet and put that away, too. The rest—the towels and floral drapes, the remaining carpet, the shower curtain, all the furniture—they took into the field and burned. The smoke was black and hung for days.

Then, nothing.

I listened for voices, for guests arguing on the walkway, for the maids in the other rooms, for their stories of Jorge and Marina and Grigorio. I saw Samuel in the parking lot once, putting a large red chest in his truck. He stood with his hands on his hips for a long time, staring. He looked right in my window.

Light became short and the rains returned, filling up the parking lot. The burned circle in the field bled, leaking black water. The sliding glass door rattled in the wind. One of the far off trees bent and did not unbend.

It was sunny again when the man in the suit came. He stood at my window. He had Mr. Kyle's face.

The floor was bare except for bits of carpet and tacks. There was still a slight darkness where Mr. Kyle had fallen. The man in the suit stared at the spot. He turned away with his hands in his pockets, shaking his head.

Two large yellow PEREZ MOVING trucks arrived. Four men stood outside my window as the man in the suit had. I heard one man with a mustache say *Qué horrible*. The others nodded and they filed away slowly. They never entered my room.

I listened to them sing and whistle as they walked backwards in pairs, filling the trucks with beds and dressers and lamps and televisions. A box full of small white bottles broke open as a man carried it, spilling blue-green liquid everywhere. The maids' cleaning carts and vacuums were loaded last. They left.

The Delta Ray Motor Inn went dark.

Sometimes people stop in the parking lot to sit on their bumpers or look at maps. They eat sandwiches and nap and their dogs pee in the weeds. I watch the traffic and the rain and the men stripping and painting the billboards, swinging in the wind.

The brown animal still comes. He sneaks along the building, his ears pointed. I saw him once, after the fire, come to the circle and walk along its perimeter, his nose to the ground. Now the black circle is becoming dead grass. There are yellow flowers where once there were none.

PHOEBUS &

PHAETHON

I knew him when we were young.
I knew his darkened eye, his sad sneer
and defiant stance.

Once, behind the library, we kissed, cool
fingers along my throat. When he beat
that boy for talking shit he didn't know
shit about (he always wore a patch
after that) I didn't see

him for a while: expelled,
cast out, all over
anger at a father more
absent than my own.

Mine said, *Good riddance.*
Saying *He deserves the truth*
earned me a constellation
of bruises.

To wonder—not to know—is worse,
though his mother always promised;
he said she said royalty:
a king, a star, a god.

Afternoons alone together, hiding
in the belly of a gutted house,
each window a face—god, king, father—
each shattered by a shameful brick.

Storm season raged that year,
left us wrung-through, blind, dark for days.
He was caught out one night, alone
on a crest, and struck:

twinned forks of lightning,
I heard, hurled from on high
lit him from within
(if you can believe it). I never

saw the body,
never said goodbye,
never thanked him
for the kiss.

hiding in the belly of
a gutted house...

AFTER THE

FUNERAL

You would be disappointed. First thing
after I get home, don't even peel out
of my black jacket and pants slick as Visqueen,
but go straight to the garage for the blue
-flared aluminum rectangle, old socket set,
lovingly shoved in a forgotten drawer.
I finger each fat-knuckled ring,
carefully consider every aperture. I weed out
the one most used, most useful to you.
Sail it, without ceremony, over the red
canyon lip, a bright wink and gone.
I'll look for it in spring when the river runs
high, fat and angry with fresh thaw. A fish eye
glinting in the bottom silt. Maybe I'll find it. Maybe
not, among the rocks. But you'd be
so proud: I hurled just like you taught:
shoulder, elbow, wrist-snap
and release.

ILLUSTRATIONS

MIGRATORY
Beth Austin
bethaustinillustration.com

MY OTHER, LONLIER BROTHER
Lea Rebecca Karlsen
tinyelephantillustrations.tumblr.com

INSOMNIA
Adriana Vawdrey
adrianavawdrey.com

PHOEBUS & PHAETHON
Autumn Northcraft
autumnroseillustration.com

AFTER THE FUNERAL
Danny Frazier
dannyglennfrazier.com

CREDITS

This is Self Titled #1.

Words by Graham Murtaugh
Layout by Zech Bard

THANK YOU
The Murtaughs, Murdock-Bairds,
Reimers and Lutzes, Martin French,
Robyn Steely, Tom Stutzman,
Josh Frankamp, Gilda Mae, Mandi
Murtaugh, Breena Bard, Charles
Bullock, Nick Cox, Toby Grubb and
Tim Kamerer.

thereisnosafety.com
grahammurtaugh.com
selftitled.co